Trains

London Underground

by Julie Murray

2

Dash!
LEVELED READERS
An Imprint of Abdo Zoom • abdobooks.com

Dash!
LEVELED READERS

2

Level 1 – Beginning
Short and simple sentences with familiar words or patterns for children who are beginning to understand how letters and sounds go together.

Level 2 – Emerging
Longer words and sentences with more complex language patterns for readers who are practicing common words and letter sounds.

Level 3 – Transitional
More developed language and vocabulary for readers who are becoming more independent.

THIS BOOK CONTAINS RECYCLED MATERIALS

abdobooks.com

Published by Abdo Zoom, a division of ABDO, PO Box 398166, Minneapolis, Minnesota 55439.
Copyright © 2022 by Abdo Consulting Group, Inc. International copyrights reserved in all countries.
No part of this book may be reproduced in any form without written permission from the publisher.
Dash!™ is a trademark and logo of Abdo Zoom.

Printed in the United States of America, North Mankato, Minnesota.
102021
012022

Photo Credits: Alamy, Getty Images, iStock, Shutterstock
Production Contributors: Kenny Abdo, Jennie Forsberg, Grace Hansen, John Hansen
Design Contributors: Candice Keimig, Neil Klinepier, Victoria Bates

Library of Congress Control Number: 2021940195

Publisher's Cataloging in Publication Data

Names: Murray, Julie, author.
Title: London underground / by Julie Murray
Description: Minneapolis, Minnesota : Abdo Zoom, 2022 | Series: Trains | Includes online resources and
    index.
Identifiers: ISBN 9781098226732 (lib. bdg.) | ISBN 9781644947258 (pbk.) | ISBN 9781098227579
    (ebook) | ISBN 9781098227999 (Read-to-Me ebook)
Subjects: LCSH: Subways--Juvenile literature. | England--London--Juvenile literature. | Local transit--
    Juvenile literature. | Transportation--Juvenile literature. | Railroad travel--Juvenile literature.
Classification: DDC 388.42--dc23

Table of Contents

London Underground

The London Underground is a **system** of rapid transit trains in England.

It is often called "The Tube" by locals.

Central London Tube map

Key to lines and symbols

▬▬▬ Bakerloo	~~Blackfriars~~	Station closed
▬▬▬ Central	○	Interchange stations
▬▬▬ Circle	♿	Step-free access from the platform to the street
▬▬▬ District	⇄	National Rail
▬▬▬ Hammersmith & City	⛴	Riverboat services
▬▬▬ Jubilee		
▬▬▬ Metropolitan		
▬▬▬ Northern		
▬▬▬ Piccadilly		
▬▬▬ Victoria		
▬▬▬ Waterloo & City		
▬▬▬ DLR		
▬▬▬ London Overground		

MAYOR OF LONDON   Transport for

Willesden Junction · Kensal Rise · Brondesbury Park · Brondesbury · Kensal Green · Queen's Park · Kilburn High Road · Kilburn Park · Maida Vale · Warwick Avenue · Paddington · Royal Oak · Westbourne Park · Ladbroke Grove · Latimer Road · East Acton · White City · Shepherd's Bush · Holland Park · Wood Lane · Shepherd's Bush Market · Goldhawk Road · Kensington (Olympia) · Barons Court · Hammersmith · Ravenscourt Park · West Kensington · Earl's Court · West Brompton · Edgware Road · Bayswater · Notting Hill Gate · High Street Kensington · Gloucester Road

The **system** is made up of more than 4,100 trains and around 250 miles (402 km) of track.

The Tube has nearly 300 stations. Most of them are in London.

Despite being called the Underground, 55% of the **system** runs above ground.

The Tube's History

The Tube began operating in 1863. It was the first underground railroad in the world!

The Metropolitan line
was the first to open
on January 10, 1863.

Many more **lines** have opened since.

The first trains used **steam engines**. They pulled wooden carriages. Beginning in 1890, electric trains were used.

INNER CIRCLE

23

One of the newest **lines** is the Elizabeth Line. It **honors** Queen Elizabeth II. Trains and ten new stations were built for it.

More Facts

- The Tube is used by more than 1.35 billion people every year!

- The average speed of the trains is 20.5 mph (33 kph).

- Thousands of Londoners used the Tube as a bomb shelter during World War II (1939-1945). They slept on the **platforms** and tracks.

Glossary

honor – to give special recognition or show respect and admiration for.

line – one of the many different lines, or railway, in a train system. Lines can be different sizes and serve different people. Some lines allow trains to move faster than others.

platform – a raised area next to railroad tracks for the boarding of trains.

steam engine – an engine that uses steam to supply energy to its mechanical parts.

system – a group of parts that work together as a whole.

Index

Online Resources

Booklinks
NONFICTION NETWORK
FREE! ONLINE NONFICTION RESOURCES

To learn more about the London Underground, please visit **abdobooklinks.com** or scan this QR code. These links are routinely monitored and updated to provide the most current information available.